Poems for Life.

A compilation of family poems

by

Magdalene N. Meduoye

CONTENTS

ACKNOWLEDGEMENTS.

I thank God for giving me the opportunity to live in a family that has allowed me to grow in love, by sharing our lives. I am sincerely grateful for the support given by my husband, Bode Meduoye. Thanks for listening to some of my ideas over and over again and consistently showing interest and appreciation. These poems are truly poems for living. They are an integral part of our lives.

I am grateful to my family for the acceptance of my uniqueness which is a key part of my journey in the writing of this book. You allowed me to fulfil my desire to make a difference in the lives of all, within the family, by EXPRESSING in words my affections and commitments to our union. As I pursued this goal, I discovered that the lessons learnt and the principles uncovered could be a great blessing to others.

Thanks for allowing me to explore my feelings and challenges in discussions and through my love letters to you. As I wrote these poems, I discovered the keys to building strong and lasting relationships within the family. You are my inspiration!

I am grateful to the friends who have been part of my journey. Thanks for the time that you spent listening to my points of view and adding to my understanding of my life and the dynamics within the family.

Thanks to Dr Arinola Araba and for her editorial work and supportive ideas during the publishing process; And to Prophet Elaine for staying up all night, two days in a row, to check the contents.

FOREWORD.

Years have gone by since I was a child. One of the things I can remember about growing up is the absence of words that showed emotions or an engagement with life, to share and solve problems.

This fact only made me more determined to ensure that I used my words to engage with my sons and other members of the family. It felt as if the gap that I experienced in my childhood, intensified my love for words and the willingness to use words to connect and extend relationships.

The poems in this book, were specifically written for my family and then I decided to share them with the world. The world awaits the harvest of goodness that can be reaped, as we choose to allow the thoughts within to be expressed in words. We need people who believe in us and are willing to tell us so, through poetry or other ways of communication.

It is time for you to let the world know how much you care through your words. There is no limit to what you can accomplish through this commitment.

These poems will enlighten, refresh and motivate you to become the best of who you can be and to be a blessing.

PREFACE.

I am grateful that you have decided to read these poems written from a heart that desires the best for our families and a better world for our children. The Lord has taught me over time, some of the keys that make this goal easier in the face of the challenges encountered by families today.

Parenting is made more challenging as the members of the family carry unresolved issues. I am convinced that communicating feelings with integrity, removes barriers to building strong and healthy homes that raise up the leaders and make a difference in our communities.

My hope is that as you read about my journey through my poems, you will be able to sit and stand where I was, while journeying with my family. This will allow you to learn some of the vital skills for successfully building your family.

In this book, I celebrate every aspect of life and encourage all the members of the family to become the best that they can be.

Enjoy the journey with me!

New Year's Eve - A Fresh Start

Reset your hope!

Refocus your goals!

Recalibrate your life!

Realign to your destiny!

Reconnect to God!

Readjust your commitment!

Reaffirm your faith!

Restart your race!

Refocus for clarity!

It is a time to give yourself a gift of a new start.

Make the best use of it!

Happy New Year

Let the sound of joy be heard!

It is a time for new beginnings.

Hear the sound of the church bells ringing loudly,

As the children and adults rejoice at the bursting forth of a new year.

Playing the harp and the loud cymbals as extravagant melodies rise.

Piercing through the doorways and the highways,

Yelling the thunderous sound of thanksgiving to God who created all things for His pleasure.

Nearer comes the beat and harmony of praise,

Extraordinary choirs dancing to the joy created through the night,

Words cannot express the joy felt by all.

You are special and the plans of God for you are exceptional,

Enter into the praise dance for we know His plans for us are good.

A loud hallelujah can be heard from willing hearts.

Rise up and dance, it is the beginning of a new year and the possibilities are endless.

Happy New Year, Everyone!

HEALING

Stand On The Word of God For Healing

God has healed you and every member of your family.

The Word of God also keeps you safe.

I am standing on the Word of God on your behalf.

God always keeps His word.

This is what I did while you and your brothers were babies.

I always believed that God would keep you safe.

I am doing the same for you and your family today.

I love you more than words can express!

"Rise and be healed in the name of Jesus!"

God's word gives healing and health.

The Power Of Thoughts

Tonight, I felt drawn to you as I was listening to a neuro-scientist's description of the power of our thoughts on our words and actions.

Remember that God has given you the ability to choose and to create innovative products that change the world.

Beneath each witty idea are capsules holding all the resources required to bring them to reality.

Endless possibilities lie ahead of you waiting to dance into the world.

Mummy knows you have all that you need, to see and maintain the pathway to realising all that is possible.

In the depth of creativity, perseverance keeps you moving forward!

God has called and equipped you with all that you need.

All that is within you is dancing in the wind of success, breakthrough and innovation.

I love you today more than I loved you yesterday!

Happy Christmas to you and your family!

Greatness Embraces Humanity

Greatness comes as we accept our humanity and inadequacies, while being confident that God in us, makes us strong.

Blow the trumpet of triumph for God in you, makes you more than enough for the next step and the next....

Each day is a treasure to be treasured even when you feel it has not been as productive as you wanted it to be.

May your life, family and the plans that you are working on, display the glory of God for all to see.

In the hands of the Lord, you are safe, loved and special.

You are a unique gemstone that continually knows that he is special and greatly loved.

A mother's heart sings over you today with joy.

Thanks for being a great blessing in our lives.

Your year will be filled with blessings beyond your wildest dreams.

Resurrection Power Working Through You

Thanks for allowing the Resurrection Power of God to work through you, as you teach and model the love, power and glory of God to your wife and sons.

Today, I give God all the glory for a life that reflects Jesus, while embracing your humanity.

I love you more than words can express!

Set Clear Goals

Live a "JUST DO IT!" life.

Specify your GOALS.

Then write a list of premise (beliefs), visions, purposes and strategies – (PVPS) that will support your goals.

Meditate on the Word of God and receive direction from the Lord.

Write down a list of actions.

"Just do It!" with passion and commitment!

Remember, ask the question - What can I do to achieve my goals today?

Inspirational Poem For You

I am so glad that you belong to this family.

We are a team and we work together to bring out the best in each other.

We forgive before acts of offence are experienced because love enables us to overlook and keep loving.

We are a team, that is destined for greatness in all areas of our lives.

The best is yet to come!!!!

Embrace God's Idea For Your Life

The day you embrace God's idea for your life, you will know it.

It may start small but it grows and becomes a phenomenon that engulfs your whole life.

It is in the place of service and giving.

The whole world awaits the manifestation of what you carry.

It takes you to a place of uniqueness and breathtaking effectiveness.

It comes when you are finally done with trying to do your own thing and you are willing to lose it all for the sake of Jesus Christ.

As you hit God's idea for your life, the artesian well breaks its confines and surges into the world that has waited for you, for so long.

Then God and you become One in Christ and all that matters is God.

Do not be afraid to let go, for as you yield so will the river be released to carry you to a land flowing with milk and honey.

Lord, I surrender and receive all that You have for me.

Hallelujah!

Sparkling In The Dark

Diamonds sparkle in the dark in the presence of the Light.

Being loved is the light that can never be dimmed.

Endless Light flows from my heart to yours.

Most of the moments that cause concern are melted in the Love that is the greatest of all, in the Light

In my heart and yours today, a radiant Light shines and dissolves all that threatens our sense of wellbeing.

Being in the Light, is the greatest gift of all.

Searching To Be

Searching relentlessly for the heart, so that I will be like Jesus, has become indelibly grafted in my will, by grace.

Looking beyond the visible, is a craving that hangs its embrace in all the hidden corners of my soul.

Recklessly living, even when it hurts, has dug a deep place of rest in my innermost being.

Seeing a rainbow in every storm, has become the dance of choice in this life that craves for God more than life itself.

Letting go of all things, so that doors to untold blessings open perpetually, is the agreed mode of action.

What a Transformation! Could only be seen as revealed by God the Source of all good things!

Thank You God for giving us all things to enjoy!

Pain Is A Friend

I discovered pain is my friend not my enemy.

In the furnace, I am positioned to see the fourth Man in the Fire

- Our Lord and Saviour, Jesus Christ.

I now know that the best gift to give to every challenge is to allow the blessings released in the furnace to take you deeper into God and finding out who you are in Christ.

Every challenge creates an environment for growth, depending on your response to it.

You know that God has set you up to win and the power to be victorious is inside you - Christ in you is the hope of glory!

Raise your eyes above the waves and there you will see and experience the empowerment of the Holy Spirit.

The next challenge will find you prepared to surf above the storm and ride the waves, to knowing God and yourself more.

Thank God for the storms.

I embrace my storms and the resistance to praise is met with a greater

commitment to Praise and Thanksgiving.

Keep your eyes on the Saviour for the storm will soon be over and you

will be left with the blessing released in the epicentre of the storm.

Thank You God for the storms of life.

Safe in Christ!

Secure in hope!

Silent and Resting!

Let it be to me according to Your word.

Declaration

The anointing to start and to finish is enabling you to work on the dreams that God has put in your spirit.

Your dreams are part of God's plan for you.

They are inside you.

God has placed on you the anointing to start and finish the projects that are linked to your dreams.

The Holy Spirit gives, grows and executes the dreams that have been given to you.

Take your dreams, especially your daytime dreams, seriously.

Commit to starting and finishing all tasks with the spirit of excellence.

Thank God for being the Giver of dreams in your life.

Keep creating and working on your dreams.

Listen Before You Move

It has to be recorded in heaven concerning both of you, that you, like

Abraham, did not move because you were persuaded that God is able to

do all things, including giving you the best mortgage deal on the market.

Listen, before you move!

Eyes Opened

The eyes of your heart are flooded with light so that you can understand

and know your business and ministry; and know through experience, the

glorious riches of His inheritance in you - a set apart one.

You are special.

Dear Lord, we thank You for opening our eyes to know how blessed we are.

God is communicating your need to many people and they are praying for you!

Good night!

Learning Through Project Life

I just want to say that I appreciate you so much.

I am so grateful to God and to you, for standing with me to see the vision that God has put in me come to pass.

I learnt so much from walking with you:

I learnt that doing a project requires a commitment to excellence.

I learnt that we must always know and experience the freedom to bring our own uniqueness and reality into the project.

I learnt that we must always be our brother's keeper each step of the way.

I learnt that we need to keep going until we find the answer that we are looking for.

Thanks for your single-minded devotion to the project.

I love you very much!

Pulled To A Quiet Place

I feel a tug is pulling me away to a quiet place with the Lord.

My whole being feels the shimmer of love from the gaze of the Saviour but yet unsure of the destination.

A voice whispered in my shaky breath, "You do not need to understand but simply follow. That is why He is God!

He is bigger and wiser than you and He knows what is best for you.

At this point I felt a sigh of relief and gently placed my hand in the hand of the Saviour.

I willingly allowed Jesus Christ to take the lead, knowing that wherever He takes me will be a bit of heaven on earth.

Suddenly, the divine carriage, with a powerful start, carried me into the sky where I joyfully looked at what I left behind.

The things faded into nothingness for I discovered they were perishable and could not withstand time.

But where the Lord was taking me was full of things that endure for eternity.

The sound of singing, clapping of excited hands and feet moving to the rhythmic sound of heaven.

This indeed is heaven! It is a place of complete surrender.

It is a place where God alone is worshipped and adored.

It is a place where nothing is hidden from the view of God who created all things for His pleasure.

It is a place where faith is no longer required, for all that God is and has can be understood by those that He had redeemed, by the Blood of the Lamb.

Wow! Home at last cried my excited heart.

Heavenly rapture filled the air!

Wow, I am home at last!

You Are A Special Son

You are like a well-watered garden that is fruitful in all seasons.

Today is a special day of blessings in your life and family.

Remember, I am the 'Mama' in a tutu, on the touchline, willing you on to victory, in all that you set your heart and hand on.

Have a richly blessed day!

Memories Are Made

Memories are made when simple acts of love are repeated and become character.

All the stars in the sky cannot hold the memories carried in our hearts.

Gentle words spoken with love.

Daring acts of kindness that change lives.

A collage of stories told with humour in all seasons.

Letting love cover a multitude of missed opportunities.

Endless joy is our portion in this family!

Never forget that love has no limit.

Enjoy the bond that holds us together as a team.

Thanks for being part of this family!

Rise And Be A Trail Blazer

To know that my accomplishments make you proud of me, is my inspiration!

I desire to be a 'trail blazer' that leaves a legacy that endures for many generations.

I look forward to you saying the same words over your son as he grows older.

You are definitely going to have great times together!

I am committed to being always in the life of your family, always!

Thanks for your love!

God Set You On A Platform

God indeed has been very good to you.

Love picked you up and set you on a platform that God alone could have created for you.

Up to the tallest skyscraper the Lord has placed you to enrich you through His intimacy with you.

With you in His arms the world becomes a place that is for growth and development.

A young man with courage, determination and love is who you have become.

Sing it out and let the whole world know that even when life throws you a lemon, with Christ you can make lemonade.

Excitement is the mother of invention because it fuels the search for solutions that are hidden deep within the heart.

Keep creating and innovating.

Under the canopy of love, which is what we hold in our hearts for you, you are complete and whole.

Never give up son, for there is always a rainbow waiting to be revealed.

You are my hero and I love you very much.

Life

Life sometimes feels like a crazy roller coaster ride.

That seems to be twisting and turning at a speed that is out of this world.

Life sometimes is like a collection of pearls encased in a dark grey clay mound.

Life sometimes is like a gently flowing river that is facing an uphill task of climbing the steep slope of a mountain.

Whatever the situations that you face, God is always on your side and He will help you.

Stretch and grab the hand of God's love.

With Him on your side, it is always well with your soul.

I Declare

I am a Pneumapreneur (Holy Spirit and Entrepreneur partnership).

I am on earth for a divine purpose.

I am created in Christ Jesus to do good works that God has prepared beforehand.

I am God's workmanship and I walk in God's good works.

I partner with the Holy Spirit to do these good works in my personal life, family, business, ministry and all my relationships, in Jesus' name! Amen!

I hear the voice of the Holy Spirit as He leads me today in all areas of my life.

Visualise

Visualise the earth yielding wealth into your hands.

Visualise money working for you and making more money.

Visualise yourself being a good manager of money.

Visualise yourself doing what you love doing most to an extraordinary standard.

Visualise all receiving your products and services and blessing you in return.

Visualise the angels of God as they minister to all your needs.

Visualise the Resurrection Power of God as it flows through you to

accomplish all that is above and much more....

Visualise a life of detachment from your goals so that you commit and do with clarity.

This is a special type of prayer -

Intentions sent forth to GOD, others, the world and self.

As you detach from it, it multiplies and grows abundantly.

I have a Millionaire mindset.

Thank You Father, Son and Holy Spirit.

Work!

'Work with your hands!' Is it a command or a choice?

On the day you wake up with no garden to tend and multiply,

you know you have abdicated your responsibility.

Reach deep down and let your deep call unto God's deep.

Kings rule and reign in their area of influence – that's who you are!

NO LAZY PEOPLE HERE!!!!!

Laziness makes people stretch and wait for handouts!

A diligent person reaches for the depth of the talents and gifts within,

to create money.

Zapping the remote control could provide short sessions of ecstasy!

You need to remember the day of reckoning is at hand.

NO LAZY PEOPLE HERE!!!!!

Deep bubble of love

Deep bubble of love, flowing from deep within, makes us people to be reckoned with.

That love turned our family into a powerhouse of encouragement and support.

It ensures we fulfil our potential with determination and courage.

That love makes us willing to listen from the heart to the needs and wants of members of the family.

That love, makes us a believer in the power within us, to reach out and to show kindness and empathy.

That love sets us apart for greatness and lives of exploits.

Today, I thank God for the gift of love that we carry.

Let it flow, for it turns our lives into a blessing to all that we meet today.

I love you today more than I loved you yesterday!

What Ifs...

What if the Lord allows us to get permission to use the church by our house to start a fellowship?

What if we are able to rent that place at a token price and God sends us into the neighbourhood, to invite people to join with us as we serve our gifts to the community?

What if you give IT courses at a nominal fee and I give coaching at a nominal fee?

What if all these activities are so filled with the Holy Ghost that miracles start happening every time we meet?

What if the announcement of the miracles begin to travel around the whole town so that a huge crowd of people queue to enter the place of meeting?

What if God, through these acts of His divine love and mercy, draws our community to Jesus?

What if this place of meeting becomes a place of revival and the growth becomes a whole community walking with the Holy Spirit?

What if God sends angels to fellowship with the congregation all the time?

What if there are always physical manifestations of God's presence in our garden?

What if knowing and experiencing the Holy Spirit as Fire, Dove, Cloud,

Light, Power, becomes the experience of all?

What if this gathering is always under an open heaven?

What if others throughout the world begin to refer to this Presence of God as the beginning of a Revival?

What if the thirst for the Word of God becomes an all-consuming passion in our lives

What if our sons become partners with the Holy Spirit as they serve God in this season?

What if God reveals His love and power to all and He alone takes all the glory?

Father, this is a long list of what ifs.

We know with God there is….

Nothing impossible.

We surrender to You. Your kingdom come and Your will be done.

We are willing, Lord help us to overcome all the blockages on the path.

Lord, we bow down and worship You - YAHWEH!!!!

The what ifs are answered with one bold declaration.

The Resurrection Power, MAKES ALL THESE BLESSINGS OURS Today!

I Am Determined

I am determined to make it, even if it is the last thing that I accomplish on earth.

I am determined to pour out all that is within me to make the world a better place.

I am determined to walk in the footsteps of the Saviour, Who set his face like a flint and refused to back down in the face of challenges.

I am determined to dance the dance that has been lunged into the INNERMOST part of my being before I was conceived in my mother's womb.

I am determined to make a difference in the world, in the service of God and humanity.

I am determined to shine in my uniqueness and brightness, that is mine and mine alone.

I am determined to continue to dance and make a difference even if nobody joins me in the dance.

I am determined to rise out of the ashes of defeat and failure and shine again and again.

I am determined to shout out to the world that the journey has just started, so make room for me!

I am determined that the hands of the past will not strangle my story.

The lukewarmness of those around will not discourage me.

The enormity of the future yet to be released will not overwhelm me.

I will dance even if nobody is watching.

I am determined for I know that in the dance is the fulfilment of my deepest cry.

I groan to give birth in the face of those dark corners that still need to be reached by grace.

I am determined!

Dream Big!

You are what you think!

Believe it - God has given you the ability to build any idea which you desire.

Exciting news - You are born rich and your abundance is contained in your thoughts.

Make being good to yourself one of your prime objectives, for you are a vessel that God has set apart for mind-blowing success and love.

In the world that you dwell in, your physical follows your dream and imaginations.

You are always and will always be a work in progress!

You are making extraordinary progress!

A loud Hallelujah rings out from us to the Lord on your behalf.

We love you today more than we loved you yesterday!

Open The Door Wide And Let The Holy Spirit Come In

Open the door wide and let the Holy Spirit come in.

When He comes in, He releases all to enter into life in freedom.

This freedom enables all to live authentically without wearing a mask.

It is the freedom that allows Jesus Christ to be released through each life.

It is the freedom that takes away all fears and replaces fear with faith.

It is the freedom that always causes all to come out of the boat and tread on the waters.

It is the freedom that causes our entire being into the oneness that is ours in Jesus Christ.

It is the freedom that makes life a never-ceasing flow of exploits.

It is the freedom that opens wide the gate so that the King of Glory may come in.

It is the freedom that makes Jesus known in all corners of the world as we surrender to the life of God within.

It is the freedom that creates a holy dissatisfaction that keeps us pressing in.

In Christ.

It is the freedom that changes our ashes to diamonds set in the flesh.

It is the freedom that makes the world a place to learn a dance that continues to eternity.

It is the freedom where the whole of life originates and dances with Divinity.

What awesome grace!

God's Glory Is Rising In Your Life

From the rising of the sun to the going down of the same, the Lord's name is to be praised.

IT IS RISING OVER YOUR LIFE.

Just as the sun rises up and brings light into lives and situations,

so is God's glory rising in your life.

God is bringing new people into your life and cutting off some others.

Friendship is a two-way thing. When friendships become one way, they begin to drain you.

They take too much from you and give very little back.

You are wearing a pair of boots and stepping up to crush the head of the enemy-

The soles of the boots are thick and jagged.

Self - Esteem

Today, I.am feeling so compassionate towards my frightened self
that is suffering from low self-esteem because of failures of the past.
I acknowledge and embrace you in your pain and I also want to
thank you for trying to protect me by avoiding attempting new things.
I just want you to know that God loves us just the way we are and so
we can choose a new thought.

We will take small steps so you do not feel overwhelmed or fearful.

I will listen to you when you start having those fears and I will see them
as indicators of a call to modify my affirmations.

I will always frame affirmations that you are comfortable with.

We will make it together.

Someday, we will no longer be afraid to try new things.

We will seek out new experiences together, for we know that stretching
ourselves promotes growth.

We are in the same team and we shall make it together, by God's grace.

Thanks for standing by me all the way.

God is for us and we are safe in His hands.

New Thought

Though I have had setbacks in my career, calling and business in the past, I am learning.

I know by God's grace that I have succeeded as a mother and a wife.

I know I can start and grow a business that uses my skills, interests, abilities and talents to add value to others by mentoring, coaching, teaching, writing and counselling.

While adding value to others, I can make money.

A Man On A Mission

You are a man on a mission to change the world!

Being committed to the dream has been a passion that kept you burning the midnight candle.

Excelling at what you do, is the desire that lubricates dreams and opens doors of opportunities.

Many of your dreams are burning through you to reality as we speak.

In the passionate pursuit of excellence, you have created pathways for others to be loved and appreciated.

God has decided to showcase His love and power through you with your partnership.

A shout of celebration can be heard as the glow of a trendsetter envelopes all that you do.

I love you more than words can express!

Passing Over

We thank the Lord for the gift that you were to your family and to the world.

Listening to how you have impacted lives fills my heart with joy to overflowing.

Unto the sky, Jesus Christ took you to stay with Him forever.

Wide open were the gates of heaven as you approached the Saviour who you loved so much.

Open melodies could be heard as you approached the presence of the King of kings.

Let the angels echo the sound of joy as we celebrate your life.

Endless peace and holy ecstasy await you in heaven with God.

Rest in peace.

There Is Nothing Wrong

There is nothing wrong with what God has created - you.

You simply have not reached the place of perfect harmony between the environment and who you are, yet...

When you get here:

You will hear the sound of joy and all that is around you will welcome your arrival.

You will feel the peace and love-filled hearts, as they partake of what you carry.

You will see the sky covered with colourful fireworks because you have opened the door to new things.

God in you is bringing you to that place, today.

Hallelujah!

Destiny, the environment and your potential are merged in a glorious dance.

We give God all the glory!

You Are My Inspiration

You are my Inspiration!

Your life gives me new and creative ideas!

You inspire me to step up and keep pushing through all barriers!

You inspire me to learn and grow rich!

You inspire me to live from the heart and continually be the best that I can be!

You inspire me to forgive and keep making a difference in the world!

You inspire me to hope for the best while facing the challenges and finding the best solutions.

You inspire me to be the best that I can be today and every day!

Thanks for being my Inspiration!

May God continually inspire you to reach heights that set you apart in the world.

Thanks for being my inspiration, my son!

Friendships Are Investments

Friendships that last are investments of a lifetime.

Reaching out to draw out the best in others is what you do best and I love doing the same!

In the midst of the pain, you listen attentively to remove some of the boulders on the way.

Endless rewards await you as you have chosen to be that friend.

Never to be forgotten are your words of wisdom and expression of love.

Deep within my heart, I appreciate your friendship in all seasons.

Thanks for being my son.

I love to encourage, inspire and celebrate the gifts that you carry.

Holding Contradictions

I love the way you hold a contradiction with tenderness while you walk your way through it, step by step.

I love the way you listen between the lines and crave to build yourself and others into the best that they can be.

I love the determination and commitment to fruitfulness and multiplication in all areas of your life.

I have learnt so much from being with you and watching the dance that never ends.

May the Lord bless you and always make His face shine upon you.

Thanks for being a great blessing to us, we really appreciate you.

Happy Father's Day

Happy Father's Day to all the Fathers in the house!

Fathers are treasures to behold and celebrate!

A loud song of gratitude brings joy to your hearts.

Thinking of all that you do is our gift to you!

Heroes and special mentors in the lives of their children.

Every act of kindness that you have shown will always fill the world with colours!

Reaching for a special melody for you on this day, is our delight!

Happy Father's Day to all of you!

Happiness Is A Choice

Happiness is a choice, not just a feeling!

It starts off as a thought and becomes a feeling that ignites actions.

Actions are the hands that cause a release of activities that turn into a deep work of grace, as they forge character.

While you continually take responsibility - character plots the way to destiny.

God has given us the ability to choose our feelings.

We can put together the recipe for the feelings that we want.

Choose feelings that enable you to create an extraordinary life!

Have a richly blessed day!

Begin today!

Gratitude Changes Everything

Gratitude changes the course of events as it opens doors to new possibilities.

Blowing the cobwebs of stress away and releasing a perfume that intoxicates with peace and blessings beyond your wildest dream.

Endless gratitude flows from the depth of the uniqueness, creativity and the love for living an extraordinary life, that you carry.

May this day be filled with love, success, happiness and fulfilment.

In the light that surrounds you, within and without, you continue to

grow and reach to heights of dreams.

Global doors of opportunities open before you today and the world celebrates the uniqueness of the solutions that you bring.

A loud sound of the cymbal can be heard as I pray and send you deeply felt gratitude today.

Thanks for being a blessing!

Ageing In Abundance

Good afternoon, Abundance Sisters!

We thank God who has given us abundance in Jesus Christ.

We declare that anything that challenges an overflow of blessings in our lives, loses its hold and leaves, in Jesus' name.

We are definitely born with the Kingdom's blessings flowing in, through and for us.

The thief comes only in order to steal, kill and destroy.

Jesus Christ came so that we may have and enjoy life and have it in abundance (to the full, till it overflows).

The Love That Radiates

His Love touches and radiates intensely from inside out.

The lid has been blown off the clay pot of alabaster oil!

The hand that poured the oil is mine and the heart that stirred the radar is mine too.

In the hand of LOVE, so amazing, so Divine, I will speak and act

with intense passion and full of grace.

This LOVE is turning my whole being into an extraordinary furnace of glory.

I am designing and creating an extraordinary life from inside out!

I surrender to the greatest LOVE of all.

I surrender to his Resurrection Power!

Every Storm Holds A Capsule

Every storm holds the capsule of the next level.

This is how you discover your gift.

What is triggered when you meet a stumbling block?

Dance until you enter into the bliss that is yours again.

Create the next great software for transforming the mundane to the spectacular.

Whatever draws you from the ordinary to the supernatural as you travel through life today, holds the key to the greatest adventure for you and a cause for celebration in the world.

Storms are breakthrough carriers, so keep pressing in!

God's Love Conquers The Darkness

Love that would not let you go.........

On the top of the volcanic lava, His love still speaks.

Voice of assurance rains through the dark ash.

Extreme darkness still shines in the embrace of Love.

Out of the mouth of the weak, the river of love still flows.

Fierce arms of grace contend continually to give safety and rest.

God's love is stronger than the storms of life.

Out of the storm flows love untold.

Dare to believe that the love of God will carry you through!

Have a richly blessed day all.

God is committed to blessing and keeping you safe!

Endless Possibilities Wait

Growing means change and growing influence.

The dreams and the pleasure of working to realise dreams, are to be appreciated.

Endless possibilities wait to be discovered.

Most memories are deliberately crafted through our choices.

In our hearts, we sense that you have built a world to celebrate.

God has made you a blessing to us!

And we are delighted to return your love with ours and much more!

We are determined, to consistently fill your hearts, with acts chosen to bless and take you higher.

Thanks for being you!

Life Is Beautiful

Life is not like collecting artwork for the Museum!

Life is to be experienced and enjoyed to the full!

It is to be designed and created with deep and careful thoughts.

(The Image of God inside you makes this possible).

Life is to be appreciated and celebrated!

Life is surely a great gift given to man by GOD!

Life and living is beautiful as you learn how to LIVE!

I hope you are blessed by it.

Growing As A Father

Growing as a father is a thrilling experience!

Being part of the script that leaves memories of joy in your son, is a gift to be cherished.

Endless opportunities to deposit exciting moments that raise a strong, independent, happy and successful son.

May each thrill change you and release great blessings into your life.

In the moment that always reminds you of how blessed you are, may your heart rise up in gratitude for the gift you carry.

You Have Scaled Mountains

You have scaled mountains.

You have left a trail that only Trailblazers can leave!

You discovered you have the power to make a difference, early!

God has filled you with so many gifts to live an extraordinary life.

I love you today more than I loved you yesterday!

The Life Of A Plant

(Family - For your enjoyment).

These plants started life as small cuttings from a far country.

A friend thought to share and they arrived to sit in small pots.

It has taken lots of tender care and love to bring out the growth that you see!

God and I worked together to produce the result.

Thank You God!

Thank you, friend!

Thank you to the hands that tended the plant!

Keep growing!

There is still a lot of scope for the endless joy that you bring!

Do not get tired of investing in your personal growth and development.

The result makes it more than worth it

Being In The Flow

I am in the flow as I play with my grandsons.

I am in the flow as I pray, praise and worship God from my INNERMOST being.

I am in the flow as I gaze into the vastness of the universe and set my mind to be lost in the AWESOMENESS GOD.

I am in the flow when I let go of life and simply CATCH the WIND and set a flight for Wonderland.

I am in the flow as I trust in God and STOP being anxious, fearful or worried.

I am in the flow when I believe that I am bearing the fruit that the Vine is producing, as I meditate on the Word of God.

I am in the flow as I pour out the vastness of love, creativity and

power of God that I carry.

I am in the flow when I know that all is well in the face of all challenges.

I am in the flow when I acknowledge that God is in the house.

I am in the flow when I believe that where I am today is the best place for me, because my steps are being ordered by the Lord.

I am in the flow as I embrace my weaknesses with joy and allow the power of God to fill me up to overflowing.

This is Eternal Life inside me.

In Jesus Christ I live in the flow consistently.

Being In A Giant Baby Bubble

Being with my grandsons is like being in a giant bubble.

In that place, nothing else in the world matters.

I have just discovered a new segment of my brain as it sparks into creative games.

In that place the wonder of being a grandmother is uncovered.

All the cares of the world fade away.

In that world, all things are possible.

In that world, every moment is fantastic and enjoyment is at its peak.

Thanks for allowing me to enjoy such splendid moments with your sons.

Those moments are safely stored in my memory to be enjoyed over and over again!

Prayer Is The Gift

Prayer is the gift that God has given to us!

Prayer is the gift that moves God to work on our behalf.

Prayer is a blessing that invites Divinity to be ever-present in our humanity.

Prayer is a call to partnership with God. to see the Kingdom of God invade the earth.

Prayer opens heaven to saturate the earth and show forth God's glory.

No wonder God said, "Men ought to pray and never give up!"

Lord, help me to pray!

FAMILY

Family That Turns Lemon Into Lemonade

Thanks for being part of the family that knows what it means to turn lemon into lemonade.

Life may give surprises but God gives the strength to make each circumstance a testimony that fills our hearts with joy.

I have watched as we continually build memories on this truth over the years and I am so grateful for each success.

Ceaseless joy floods my innermost being as I recall our journey so far.

Looking ahead to a future full of memories that leaves the whole of our being gasping for more of the best that God has for us.

Thank you, family, for being the dream maker crew!

The gift that we share cannot be bought with money but is worth more than words can express.

You are surely my motivation to be the best that I can be.

I want to make you smile and to be proud of me.

I want you to remember each moment we share with a smile on your face.

I want you to soar to heights that fill hearts with a sense of wonder!

I just want you to know the love that will never give up but keeps pushing through.

Today is surely a mirror into the glorious future that awaits each of us.

God has surely blessed us and for this we are very grateful.

Thanks for being part of the family that turns each lemon into lemonade, sells it and produces a reward!

You are my hero and I celebrate each of your accomplishments and give God all the glory!

Poem For New Month

A new Month is an opportunity to make a fresh beginning.

Up comes the overflow of colours, to make new artwork in lives and situations.

Greater hopes and dreams are yours this month!

Untold surprises await you from unusual places, as you commit to building skillfully.

Special times to be created and enjoyed as we lavishly share our love and turn our dreams into reality.

Thanks for making this month the best ever!

You are greatly loved by us!

Happy New Year Family!

Most of the steps that you will take this year will be made in the secret place.

Endless joy and peace await those who find their purpose and live it out.

During the walk through the new year, may you know the strength that comes from knowing that the family team is willing you on.

Up the heights as you scale, may you discover love and peace beyond your wildest dreams.

Open wide your heart to the endless possibilities and opportunities that are yours each moment of this new year.

You are specially wired to succeed in all that you do.

Exciting times are yours, for the Creator of the world calls you His own.

Make The Best Use Of Your Season

The season is out of your control but what you make of it is within your control.

The end can be specified while you become exceptionally creative in the season.

A lot of joy awaits those that recognise the season and make the best of it.

So, the heart of love grabs and works the season for the good of all!

On the mountain top, celebrate your harvest in this season!

Never holding back your best from all that surround you.

Whatever blessings we harvest today, it is a case of One-for-all-all-for-one.

Each individual acts for the benefit of the group - and the group acts for the benefit of each individual.

Thanks for being a part of this family.

Families Are For All Seasons

Families are for all seasons.

An endless flow of support and encouragement to rise and become the best of you.

Many challenges are successfully overcome, with words of encouragement and unflinching commitment to love and share.

In all that we give, we love without limit.

Let all that is within us flow into the hearts of all, to ease the strain that we feel sometimes.

You are part of the ever-living and growing family.

A Poem For The Family

We are a team!

Teams are built out of a love that is standing steady, in all seasons.

Teams are built out of a commitment that desires the best for one another.

Teams are built from a heart filled with forgiveness and a desire to start again with respect and honour.

Teams are built from a desire to give without a sense of entitlement.

Teams are built by little acts of kindness that leave a reservoir of memories.

Teams are built with words that cannot but bless and leave a smile in the heart and on faces.

Teams are what make the world that we live in so meaningful and memorable.

Remember, we are a team and we are in it for love!

Thanks for being a member of this team!

Declarations Over Your Family

Today, you develop skills, gifts and abilities for industry or commercial activities.

Today you live a brave, interesting and fun-filled life.

Today, you do notable deeds or feats, especially those that are God glorifying and heroic.

Today, you make the best use of all the natural and supernatural resources that you have.

Today, you do acts of remarkable brilliance, daring and bold.

Today you use all that you have productively.

Today, you stir up interest in projects that promote profitability in your areas of productivity.

Even in this season, you continue to live lives of Exploits!

Endless Possibilities For A Glorious Day

Today, is the best day of our lives because we have all the possibilities for a glorious day, ahead of us.

The choices that we make determine the outcomes.

Families that choose to love, build a strong foundation that enriches all.

Families that choose being there, in the wind and rain, choose strength and prosperity.

Families, that choose to see the best in each other, choose to enable the best in each of us, to flow and make a difference in the world.

We are a family, so loving each other, comes in every word and action.

Learning To Love

Loving you is a delightful experience!

Through you, I learnt that being loved and loving others has great value.

It allows the heart to skip with joy.

It puts sparkles in the deepest part of our being!

It opens us to all the fantastic things that are for us to share!

It makes us confident as we stride into the day to live fully!

Love is indeed a power tool for life!

Thanks family, for giving and receiving love beautifully!

We are loved! May that thought make your heart dance in the sunlight.

Love is what it is all about!

We celebrate being a family!

The Child Any Parent Would Love

You are the daughter that any parent would love to have!

You are my princess and strong soldier!

You are the light and salt of any relationship!

You are the delightful sunshine on a hot summer's day, filling the world

with light.

You are the intentional lover that seeks to fulfil the best that is deep within!

You are the choreographed dance that can only be understood by God and you.

You are the potential being revealed through every dark night of the soul and in the colourful rainbow of day.

You are the lover that gives all and gets abundance in return.

No seed sown through your life ceases to yield abundance.

You are special and in the canopy of Love, all is well!

Keep dancing my daughter.

Take responsibility for the next design and creation!

You can do it, for God has given you all that you need!

Dance, Dance! Dance!

Creating A Fragrance

Fun-filled family bonds, create a fragrance that reaches far and wide.

All that can be heard, are the footsteps of love, creativity and forgiveness!

May our lives together, encourage us individually and collectively, to reach for the stars!

In the thick of the uncertainties that life throws at us, we continue to turn our lemons into lemonade!

Let it be known, we are a family that is committed to building our relationships, with joy and heartfelt gratitude!

You are part of this amazing relationship.

We bring the best of who we are to the table!

A Family Of My Dreams

We are so thankful for your love and friendship.

We are becoming the family of my dreams.

It is a relationship with opportunities for deep connections.

We explore experiences, share insights, support each other's growth and nurture each other's spirit.

What a family!

Thanks for being part of this family!

Thanks for the video call!

Thanks for your greetings.

Thanks for being willing participants in my moments of uncontrollable joy.

We are indeed surrounded by fascinating people!

The Family That Dances With The Storm

This family is committed to getting through the fiercest storm by praying and trusting in God, to guide us each step of the way.

We encourage one another to rise and climb up to heights, beyond their wildest dream, for we know we are wired for success.

When we slip, we undergird the fall, to ensure that we learn, and very soon start climbing again.

We are believers in one another's ability to make a difference in the immediate and wider family.

We know that good things happen to those who keep working out each step, for the resolution of problems and bringing out the best, in all that we do.

We know that the dance goes on, but the best dance moves are for us as we think and grow richer in all that we do.

I hold you up today as carriers of peace, love and abundance, by God's grace

Thanks for being a part of this family.

Dream For The Family

Dreaming about our family fills me with glee and I want to love you more and more!

I dream that this month will be the month of fulfilment of your deepest desire!

I dream that you will build memories in your homes that create momentum for great achievements and effective contributions to the world.

I dream that we will continually build relationships that grow stronger with time.

May you know the joy of being loved by the family and loving others, today and every day!

Super Mother

Mother!

On those cold and dark nights, you are there providing warmth through your smile and embrace.

Thanks for all that you do and who you are.

Higher than the clouds is the love of your children for you.

Endless joy is yours as God continues to pour His love into your heart.

Rest in the strong arms of the Father.

He continues to make you a light in the family and beyond!

Thanks for being Mother!

Prayer For You This Morning

I took you to the presence of the Lord this morning to pray for you, as led by the Holy Spirit.

I saw you restricted in your actions and I decreed your release.

I saw you coiled up with a feeling of disappointment and I declared an open door and wings to fly as an eagle.

I saw you with weak hands and eyes fixed on the Lord. I declared strength that is beyond what you can ask or think.

I saw you walking slowly and I decreed a release of power in your inner man that causes you to accomplish with ease all that God has put inside you.

I saw you radiating the glory of God and I heard the voice of angels shouting

'Overflow.'

I looked a bit closer to hear and see what the Lord was doing.

I saw you surrounded by the glory of God.

I saw you walking hand in hand with Jesus.

I saw you shining like the sun in its fullness. It is the glory of the Lord!

My Son, your choice to follow Jesus has made you a recipient of all that God is and has.

Have a richly blessed New Year with your special friend and wife.

This is not just a poem, I saw, heard and felt all the above at the Throne of Grace concerning you.

I thank God for His love for you and your wife.

You are greatly loved by the Lord.

A Message From a Special Friend

One day I had a special visitor who told me some amazing things about you.

He told me that you were very special to Him.

He told me that He has got a Book of Remembrance of all your acts of kindness.

He told me that He was watching over you to bless you in all that you did.

He told me that though storms would come sometimes, you would always be safe in the Rock.

He told me that your acts of kindness towards me would always be remembered and rewarded.

He showed me your glorious future that is filled with blessings beyond your wildest dreams!

MINISTRIES

Poem For Women In God's Presence

Almighty God, we adore you for the realisation of how much we are loved!

Women....

In Your presence, we are brought to the place of surrender, and in that place we are led to seek and serve the Lord.

I see the cloud of glory filling us to overflowing.

Catch the visions and write them down for He is visiting us afresh to usher in His glory.

I see the cloud of glory filling us to overflowing.

God's plans for us are being carried by the love of God into all areas of our lives and the presence of God is bringing refreshment, renewal and strength.

It is raining over us and all we can do is stretch our drenched beings in His presence, in adoration.

This is a season of unusual excellence, love, power and glory for all of us.

I am so glad God brought you into my life!

LOVING

A Synchronised Dance Of Lovers

As I feel your heartbeat and mine, synchronise to a glorious dance, in all that concerns us, my heart jumps for joy.

Let love begin to radiate through actions that release hope, create dreams and bring the glorious promises of GOD into REALITY.

There is definitely no mountain that love cannot climb.

There is no valley that the bond of affection cannot cross.

There is no desert that cannot be turned into a lush garden with Agape love.

It is the love that will never let us go.

Keep dancing with me, my lover and my friend.

In this embrace of love your weaknesses and mine are turned into rockets of flashing successes.

In them, we experience the power of God to do the impossible - love a sinner saved by grace alone.

Let us hold on to our dreams and let the dance continue.

The glee can be felt by all that join the glorious worship of the Giver of all good things.

DANCE! DANCE! DANCE

Thanks For The Gift

Thanks for the gift!

May the Lord bless you abundantly with the anointing to make money; manage money and make it grow; save money and grow in financial abundance.

The Lord richly blesses you and your family with your deepest heart's desires.

May your lives overflow with wisdom, understanding, strength and counsel.

We love you more than words can express.

You Are My Valentine!

Happy Valentine's Day.

Voices of joy sing from heaven above as we celebrate this special day together.

A love that has grown stronger with the years is our experience.

With God at the centre, it has been a memorable journey.

A love that is so strong that it holds our whole being tenderly and sweetly

in the presence of the Lord, in thanksgiving.

Let us remember the wonder of being in each other's heart has been a gift that has matured with age, unabated.

Excitement, joy, gladness and untold stories of appreciation fill my heart as I remember you.

Never to be forgotten are the times of laughter; times of sharing our political debates with passion that can only be compared to the joy of finding that we are precious and unique.

Time to say thank you for being my lover and my friend…

Thanks for not holding back on loving me.

Thanks for being my special dance partner.

Thanks for making it easy to appreciate you and dance with you through the seasons and the times.

In this special moment I take time to thank God for the love that binds us together.

You are more to me than you can imagine.

Nearer my lover and friend,

May we be drawn together as the days pass by.

You are so sweet and special and I love you.

Excellent memories being built in our own unique ways!

I look forward to more splendid times ahead.

Thank you, my lover and my friend. May your day today be filled with all that you desire and much more.

Happy Valentine's Day!

A Daughter's Response To Love

Thank you for your love and your kindness and thank you for always being there to reach out.

I pray huge blessings over your life.

May you receive all that you are praying for and more.

You are one superwoman - when I look at you, I see a superwoman.

You might ask why superwoman? The reason is simple; you are always there for everyone.

You might feel tired but will not show it, for you carry a lot of peoples' cares.

You are a mum, a friend, a pillar.

Thank you so much for all you do for me and every person who has ever crossed your path.

You are one outstanding woman.

I love you mom.

Valentine's Day For My Saviour

Voicing my love for You leaves me passionately lost in Your embrace.

A love that reaches the innermost part of my being and releases joy unspeakable.

Loving You by the power of the Holy Spirit, is one of the greatest joys of my heart.

Endless songs keep flowing out of my heart to You, my Saviour, Lover and Friend.

Nearer my heart yearns to be, higher my whole being longs for Your embrace of Love.

Time has made the love that we share stronger than ever before.

In this holy moment of this expression of love, I just want to say, I love you Saviour, more than life itself.

Never to be parted from your love and always abiding in this colourful ecstasy of joy.

Exciting times today and every day.

My Lover and my God, I worship You!

Happy Valentine's Day, Saviour!

A Poem For My Daughter

I feel like writing a poem just for you.

Happy days exist in every cloud, when we see Jesus in the raindrops.

A million voices and words cannot express the depth of love that binds us together.

Reaching out to God to receive the love that we share is a delight.

Let us keep pressing into LOVE Who is the Saviour of the world.

Enter in my daughter for you are loved more than you think.

Never give up on the power of God's love to change you and your family for good today.

Excitement is the sound that I hear as I thank God for His love for you and my love for you.

Sweet sleep my daughter!

Ceaseless Stream Of Love

Son, you are precious and greatly loved by God and I.

A ceaseless stream of joy, peace and wholeness fills you up to overflowing today.

You are special and always loved.

We are praying and loving you and your family more and more!

Just To Say - Thank You

Thanks for surrendering your life to Jesus.

Thanks for not giving up on you in the face of your weaknesses.

Thanks for being a man of integrity even when you know you are working with limited information.

Thanks for being willing to learn to love with the heart.

Thanks for doing most of our shopping with peace and love.

Thanks for allowing me to fulfil my assignment while you love and pray for me.

Thanks for solving my computer challenges.

I love and appreciate you and am still committed to finding new ways to say thank you.

May the Lord bless you today more than your wildest dreams.

Here we are!

We have been on this journey for more than 40 years

Thank You Lord for everything!

Horizon Filled With Love

The horizon is filled with laughter, peace and joy when we come together.

We are memory builders and relentlessly we encourage one another to reach for the stars.

The overwhelming thought is that we are here to bless and add value to all.

Thanks for being part of this family!

My Heart Is Drawn To You

I hear your love for me through the laughter and sometimes through the silence.

Being a mother has and would always be the best gift that I could give to you.

Entering into your world authentically with my heart is what I want to give to you always.

Most of the skills that you share with me on this pathway have been learnt through your own experience.

Thanks for soldiering on to grasp the fulfilment of your authentic self.

I take responsibility for ensuring that all that you do is held in a secret place in my heart with love and tenderness.

You are a great father, partner and son.

Please keep honouring your authentic self.

A million choruses of thank you are not enough to express how I feel about you.

Thanks for holding me up when it felt that I needed you to prop me up.

Thanks for being there!

The Melody Of Worship

When I hear the melody of your heart in worship, I feel the fire of God.

When I hear the rhythm of the words of praise as it rolls out of your heart, I bow in adoration to the Living God.

Worship is a means and an end in itself.

It is a 'means' because it brings all into the presence of the Living God, Who created All things.

It is an 'end' in itself because it is the presence of God with man revealed.

Thanks for allowing God to worship through you.

You are a great blessing to us and the world.

Today, I took you and your wife to the Lord and cried – "Be glorified in their lives, Lord!"

I love you today, more than I loved you yesterday!

Thanks for your gift of love.

A Light On A Hill Top

I felt drawn to you this morning so I prayed for you.

Today, you are like a light set on the treetop.

Today, you are like a treasure-chest that contains pearls of great price.

Today, you are surrounded by favour and love.

Today, you are walking in victory and advancing to greater and greater heights!

Today, I know God loves you and we love you too.

You are a treasure and we are privileged to be your parents

Thanks for loving us!

BIRTHDAYS AND NEW MONTHS

40th Birthday Poem

Words sometimes are inadequate to describe the depth of love and appreciation that we have for you.

Unusual blessings will be the hallmark of your new year, as we celebrate every moment of the last 40 years.

May the glory of God envelope you and cause all that you touch to be a spectacular display of God's presence and power.

In this tide of well wishes, we hold you up before the Throne of Grace and ask that the Lord would continually bless and show you His love that cannot be exhausted.

Mother of three handsome young men. The anointed wife of our son.

Enter into the cloud of thanksgiving as we sing a loud hallelujah to God, on your behalf.

During the changing seasons of life, you will remain steadfastly in His blessings.

Under the wings of the Lord, you will find refuge and nourishment that sets you apart consistently in God's favour.

Open wide your heart for the release of the special blessings that are being poured out and brought to you by angels.

You are a special daughter and may the next 40 years be more glorious than the years that have just rolled by.

February

February is a month of freedom from fears, worry and anxiety.

Enter in and hear the Lord speaking to dispel all your fears, worries and anxieties.

Be reminded of the sacrifice that He made for you. He took you first to the place that has written on the doorpost, "It is FINISHED."

Reach out in praise for eternal victory over sin, Satan, death, hell and all other enemies of your life! Victory was won at Calvary.

Under the canopy of grace, His broken body and shed Blood was for the Healing of your body, soul (mind, emotions, will and conscience) and spirit.

You are fully healed and restored.

A loud Hallelujah arises, for Greater is He that is in you than he that dwells in the world.

Roll out the anthem of adoration and thanksgiving. Today, Jesus Christ dwells in you and the Holy Spirit is working in you, to execute the fullness of blessing that is yours.

Yell out the words: "February is a Month of the Release of the fullness of God's Blessings, as I receive and rest in the finished work of JESUS CHRIST!"

I declare you are:

Blessed

Restored

Rich

Rightly positioned for victory today and every day.

I love you today more than I loved you yesterday!

A New Month

Who determines the level of happiness in a new month?

Who desires that I have an extraordinary month?

Where does a happy new month begin?

Why do I want to be happy?

What are the things that make me happy?

When do I need to exercise control over self to align it to my vision and direction?

Do the changes that I make in my life this new month, have to be big to be effective?

How do I identify what and who needs to be part of my journey this month?

Can I create a vision and purpose for an extraordinary month?

Why do I need the support of self in order to create and manifest a happy, successful and extraordinary new month?

Am I responsible and accountable to God for this new month?

What is my premise for this new month?

What are the effects of respecting and honouring who I am in this new month?

Does God want me to have an extraordinary new month?

If having a happy new month was just wishes, judging by the amount of

good wishes today, we should all be mega successful, happy and fulfilled.

There is something missing in the recipe – PVPS - premise, vision, purpose and strategy.

What do you believe?

I believe that the potential for having an extraordinary month is for all but manifests to those who know and do (actively plan out) their path.

Life is full of infinite possibilities and each person builds his/her own future as they mix commitment to 'DO' into the recipe.

The sky is the limit to what I can do this month as I use my gifts and talents in the service of all.

God has given me all that I need for life and godliness.

I live with the mindset of a person who has it all and has the ability to manifest continually.

My most important question this month is - What do you want?

Dig deep to find the answer and then DO IT!

Vision For The Month

I am the driver of all that happens in this new month.

I create all the changes that will happen this month because God has

made me to commit to making my "I will", God's "I WILL."

I will live a life of 100% commitment to following the Holy Spirit Who lives inside of me.

I strive to create the breathtaking vision of who I am, what I am doing,

who I am doing it with and where I am.

Heaven will come down this month, in Jesus' name.

To be a model to my sons of what it means to live a happy, fulfilled and successful life.

To showcase the glory of God to the whole earth.

To create money by focusing on the application of spiritual rules

to all areas of my life, and thereby attract money into my life abundantly.

I will be a testament to the Truth that is in the Word of God.

I will focus on my personal development and growth and the application of what is learnt.

I will continually focus on changing my behaviour and attitude.

I have a Millionaire mindset.

Happy Father's Day

Happy first year as a father!

I cannot thank God enough for bringing your lover into your life and for giving you your special son.

Being a father has added a greater depth to your thinking and a twinkle in your eye.

Entering into the guild of fatherhood extends you to the moon and back.

Many more years of joy as you see this little extension of you grow and bring you untold joy.

In this moment, words fail me as I celebrate your first year as a father.

Giving love has a way of yielding multiples of what was given.

Endless joy and peace rolled into one, continually be yours.

Have a richly blessed day!

Happy Birthday

A day to recall the glory of God in your life.

We are glad that God gave you to us, 39years ago.

You are making a difference in the world around you. You are original, unique and definitely cannot be rivalled, in the living of a life

that has brought so much joy to all.

Open up your heart to receive all the gifts that we bring.

They are packaged in boxes ready to be delivered on your birthday!

Thanks for being a special husband, father and son.

Kind words are falling like snowflakes.

Up in the sky, the sound of aeroplanes release a colourful confetti of celebration.

We hear melodies of the gift that you are to all of us.

No words can fully express how much we love you!

You occupy a special place in our hearts.

You are always cherished and appreciated.

Letting this moment speak of how special you are, is a great joy!

Excitement, joy and laughter echo all around you, today.

Thanks for being a special son and

Happy Birthday!

Happy Birthday

YOU ARE SPECIAL!

On this special day - your 40th birthday, I chose to camp at the Throne of Grace, to celebrate the blessings and riches that are yours in Christ.

Let the sound of joy, peace and purpose be heard from the deepest part of your being.

Up in the sky, I hear the melody of Angels, that are bringing gifts beyond your wildest dreams, into all areas of your life.

Words cannot express the deep sense of love and gratitude that we have received, as we watched you grow and become who you are today.

A thousand words, stringed together in a rich melody, is not enough to tell you how much we love you.

You have always been unique and original in your thinking, actions and your delight in walking with Jesus.

Enter into the greatest joy ever as you celebrate this 40th birthday with friends and family.

Giving to you, on this special day, from a reservoir of love that can never run dry, is a delight.

Up on the mountains and the hills, a loud celebration fills the world.

Never let the celebration cease, for you were sent to the world to make a difference.

Happy Birthday!

Happy Birthday

You are blessed beyond words.

On the mountaintop, your friends celebrate with musical instruments, making melodies that reach near and far.

So another year has passed!

What memories! What celebrations!

Hear the sound of laughter as God reminds you of how special you are!

Up the hills and mountains we climb this morning to celebrate this day with you.

A loud Hallelujah we give to God as He blesses you today with blessings that raise you higher than you can ever dream!

Happy Birthday!

Special

Loved

Appreciated

Blessed "For God so loved the world that He gave His only begotten son that whosoever believes in Him will not perish but have everlasting life.". John 3:16

ABOUT THE AUTHOR

Magdalene Nkechi Meduoye is a retired school teacher. She is a Mums Must Pray Group Leader, Personal Growth and Development Coach. Her interest is in Prayer and the Prophetic and how God uses these gifts to build a strong, healthy church and family.

The words in this poem are powerful since they are linked to deep rooted thoughts. In this book, you are invited to enter into the fascinating world of words that stir feelings; invite a careful engagement with life to resolve issues; words that harness deep rooted desires and map the way ahead in relationships and these poems create a passion for life.

The poems have been divided into sections so that each section becomes a world to be explored. The poems lend themselves to being read aloud or read in silence. They can be read in a group or for a larger public audience.

The pleasure experienced while sharing the poem is beyond words. Indeed, it is better experienced than talked about.

Printed in Great Britain
by Amazon

42266465R10067